I0500690

FOLLOW YOUR FRIENDS!!

@3RdRockHipHop

Discover Music at **www.3RdRockHipHop.com**

FOR MORE INFO: 3RDROCKHIPHOP@GMAIL.COM

TABLE OF CONTENTS

INTRODUCTION..v

CHAPTER #1: PICKING UP TRASH WITH T-CAN............................03

CHAPTER #2: COLLECTING RECYCLABLES WITH BIG BINNY.........09

CHAPTER #3: TRAXX AND THE LANDFILL....................................17

CHAPTER #4: THE BEACH..29

SCHOOL RECOGNITION..41

3rd Rock Hip Hop is dedicated to using music to increase kids awareness and importance of sustaining the environment.

Introduction

In 2006, Archie Hill, a recording and performing rap artist was first approached by a friend and member of the Sierra Club who challenged him to write a rap song about saving the environment, while still making it sound cool enough for kids to actually enjoy! Jumping at the challenge, Archie created his first environmental rap song entitled "Think Green." Our team, then went on to attend several Earth Day events, and because of all the positive feedback, we decided to go green with the hip hop style of music.

"I saw so many kids at these events and it dawned on me... the kids are the future, so why not send the message of environmental awareness to them as early as possible?"

- Archie Hill

With Rap/Hip Hop being such a huge part of youth culture today and used in all forms of advertisement and media - we figured it would be the ideal format to relay the message of saving our environment to the hearts and minds of our youth!

This is where the concept of 3rd Rock Hip Hop was born!

Author: Archie Hill

Illustrator: Tobias Gebhardt

Editor: Rhonda Phillips

Layout & Design: Warren Dickson

ISBN-13: 978-1519324917

The Adventures Of 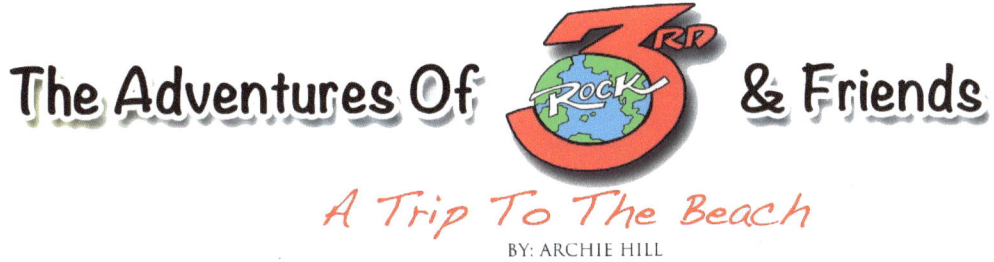 & Friends

A Trip To The Beach

BY: ARCHIE HILL

PICKING UP TRASH WITH T-CAN

Our environmental friend 3rd Rock starts out on an adventure. His little sister Lil Rock, always loves to hang out with her big brother, so he takes her along for the trip. Because its such a nice day, they decide to walk to the beach. As they go on their way, all they can think about is jumping into the cool water to go for a swim.

On the way to the beach, they run into their cool friend T-Can, who sometimes smells funny when his can is full. 3rd Rock says, "What's up T-Can?" T-Can says, "Oh nothing much, just collecting trash from the side of the road and keeping the environment clean. You know the regular routine. What are you up to?" "We're on our way to the beach, Woohoo!" Lil Rock says with excitement. "That sounds like a lot of fun," T-Can replies. 3rd Rock asks, "Would you like to join us?" "Hmm…not today, says T-Can. You know my favorite thing to do is pick up trash and keep the world looking beautiful. If we don't pick it up, it will end up in our storm drains and eventually in our ocean." "Wow, I want to help keep the environment clean too," says 3rd Rock. "Me too," says Lil Rock.

They all begin to pick up trash until the road is clean and beautiful. Once they are done, T-Can looks over at his two friends and smiles. "Thanks a lot for helping me," T-Can says. "You're welcome T-Can," says 3rd Rock and Lil Rock. "Have a nice day." T-Can moves on to clean up the rest of the neighborhood while 3rd Rock and Lil Rock continue on their adventure.

COLLECTING RECYLABLES

WITH BIG BINNY

As our friends stroll along, they see their good friend Big Binny collecting objects from the road. 3rd Rock says, "What's up Big Binny, how are you?" Big Binny replies, "I'm Awesome!" 3rd Rock says, "Lil Rock and I were just helping T-Can pick up trash from the road. Can we help you, too?" "Sure, but this isn't trash," says Big Binny. "This is what's called recyclables." "Re -Re - Recyclables?" asks Lil Rock with a puzzled look on her face. "Yes, recyclables," Big Binny answers.

"A recyclable is an old item that can be made into something new. I'm talking about things like plastic bottles, aluminum cans, paper and glass items", Big Binny explains. "I have a cool song about recycling called "Pick it up." I'll rap it for you while we pick up all the recyclables from the ground." Okay, great!" says Lil Rock with excitement.

As they enjoy Big Binny's song, 3rd Rock and Lil Rock help pick up every recyclable item they can find, until there is none left on the road and Big Binny is so full— his lid won't close well. Big Binny then glances up at his full load and says, "Thanks! So when you find recyclables lying around, collect them and give them to me. By doing this, you'll also help reduce the amount of trash we produce, which will end up in a landfill." "We will," says the two, but, what's a landfill?

"A landfill is a gigantic hole in the ground that's about the size of a baseball field," says Big Binny. "This is where all of our trash goes after we throw it away." "Wow!" Lil Rock exclaims. "That's not cool. I'm going to recycle everything I can to reduce the amount of trash that goes to the landfill." "Me too," says 3rd Rock. "Thanks for telling us about recycling and for sharing that cool song with us," he says. "Thanks for listening" Big Binny replies, as he starts to roll away.

TRAXX AND THE LANDFILL

As 3rd Rock and Lil Rock continue walking down the road, they start to notice a strange smell in the air. Lil Rock turns to 3rd Rock and frowns, "Ewww! What's that smell?" 3rd Rock replies, "I don't know what it is, but it's getting stronger."

As they go over a hill, they notice a sign that says, "Landfill Ahead." After learning about landfills from Big Binny, they're interested in learning more, so they venture on.

When they arrive at the landfill, 3rd Rock and Lil Rock can't believe their eyes and are amazed by what they see. A mountain made of trash! As they stood there gazing, a big bulldozer with a look of frustration on its face approached them (Grrrum chukka chukka, Grrrum chukka chukka). "My name is Traxx," he rumbled. "I work here in the landfill." "Hi Traxx, I'm 3rd Rock and this is my little sister, Lil Rock." Lil Rock looks concerned. "Mr. Traxx, why do you seem so sad?" she asks. Traxx replies, "Well, I work hard at the landfill every day and no matter how hard I work, there always seems to be the same amount of trash again the next day. At this rate, I think I'll have to work forever." "Well," says 3rd Rock, "we just learned about recycling from our friend Big Binny and we're going to do our part by recycling all the recyclable things we can find. That should help a little, right?" "Yes it will, but you should also reduce and reuse before you recycle," Traxx explains.

"To 'reduce', means people should only take as much of any item as they need. For example, when you grab some napkins at your favorite restaurant or you're some place that allows you to take as many items as you want, only take as many as you need. This way, the extras won't go to waste. Waste equals trash."

"Oh, okay, we get it now," says 3rd Rock. "We won't take what we don't need anymore, but what does 'reuse' mean?" "Reuse means to take an item that was used for one thing in the past and then use it for something else later," Traxx explains. "An example would be when you take a used plastic container–wash it and reuse it as a bowl, or a bank for your coins...or even a place to keep your crayons. When you're completely done using it, then it can be recycled."

"That makes a lot of sense, Traxx!" exclaims 3rd Rock. "I'm really glad we met you and learned all this cool stuff! Hopefully, we can do enough so you don't have to work so hard." "That would be great!" Traxx roars. "Thanks for all your help." "And remember to tell everyone you know to reduce, reuse, and then recycle." "We will," Lil Rock says. "Take care Mr. Traxx." Traxx goes back to work and 3rd Rock and Lil Rock continue on their way to the beach.

THE BEACH

3rd Rock and Lil Rock finally arrive at the beach. As soon as they see the water, they cheer with excitement. "Yippee!" Lil Rock says to 3rd Rock, "Let's go swimming!" They both take off their shoes, run towards the water, and dive in (Splash). 3rd Rock and Lil Rock feel really good about everything they've learned today, and because they've worked so hard to keep the environment clean, the swim is well deserved...but their adventure is not over yet.

All of a sudden, as they begin to swim, they see a furry little animal beside them. 3rd Rock smiles and says, "Hi, my name is 3rd Rock and this is my little sister, Lil Rock. How are you?" "I'm just keeping cool," the little animal responds. "Thanks for asking. My name is PC Otter. I'm a Pacific sea otter and I live in the Pacific Ocean." "Wow, you must love living at the beach," says Lil Rock. "You get to go swimming every day!" "Yeah, it's pretty nice," PC Otter says. "But sometimes the water gets very dirty and polluted with trash. It comes in from the storm drains…and it's not good for me and the other animals that live here."

"How many other animals live in the ocean?" asks Lil Rock.

"There are lots of other fish and mammals that live in the ocean," explains PC Otter. "Sometimes we might see a piece of trash and think that it's food. If we eat it, we can get very sick. This is the only reason I don't like living in the ocean." "We understand the importance of picking up our trash," says 3rd Rock. "Today we learned a lot about how the trash from the city can end up in the ocean."

"Really?" PC Otter says surprised. "That's right!" 3rd Rock replies proudly. "Our friend T-Can explained, that if we don't pick up the trash from the city, it can get into the storm drains and end up at the beach. Our other friends, Big Binny and Traxx, taught us the importance of reducing, reusing, and recycling to lessen the amount of trash we create. Now being here and talking with you really shows us how it all ties in together."

PC Otter says, "I'm very happy to know that you are helping out, but, if we're really going to make a difference, everyone's going to have to participate." "You're right, Mr. Otter," says Lil Rock. "3rd Rock and I will continue to do our part and spread the word about all the cool things we've learned today." "Thanks a lot", PC Otter replies. "That really makes me and all the other animals that live here very happy. Now, let's have fun and go for a dip." "Yaaaeee!", Lil Rock cheers. Then PC Otter joins 3rd Rock and Lil Rock for a nice swim and enjoys the ocean and sunshine.

Www.3rdRockHipHop.Com

WORD SEARCH

WORD LIST

X N E J L A N D F I L L R A Z
I V X R E D U C E C P M P J Z
O O D K C R V R E C Y C L E S
O X T A O E T S Y W Q N S M F
P F E A T U A K B T I P S D T
B U O O A S P G R E E N I Q B
S Q J Y N E V U T A A D F P O
B I G B I N N Y Z R T C F C T
D C B D P R M R L Y A J H O T
P Q X H T R A X X I C S U T L
S G T E X F J M I K L J H T E
T M M M K X R G I N E R C E S
C C F R I E N D S O A D O R C
Z G A N U M L B W F N H H C Y
T P X N N S S E H Q M U I D K

REDUCE
TCAN
TRAXX
CLEAN
REUSE
GREEN
BOTTLES
PCOTTER
LILROCK
BIGBINNY
BEACH
LANDFILL
RECYCLE
FRIENDS
TRASH

List of schools in the Los Angeles area where 3rd Rock has performed:

1. Grand View ES
2. Pennekamp ES
3. Manhattan Beach MS
4. American Martyrs ES
5. Jane Addams MS
6. Leuzinger HS
7. Kelso ES
8. Berendo MS
9. John Muir ES
10. Thomas Starr King MS
11. David Starr Jordan MS
12. Franklin Classical MS
13. Cesar Chavez MS
14. Will Rogers MS
15. Lou Dantzler Prep. ES
16. Hudnall ES
17. Worthington ES
18. Payne ES
19. Carthay Center ES
20. Leo Politi ES
21. Magruder MS
22. Vista Del Valle ES
23. Parras MS